LIMOUSINES

TRACY NELSON MAURER

Rourke

Publishing LLC

Vero Beach, Florida 32964

www.rourkepublishing.com

Project Editor
Ed Newman, AMSOIL INC.

Also, the author extends appreciation to Michael L. Bromley, the editorial staff of *Limousine Digest*, J.J.'s Limousines, Bill Bishop, Tecumseh Trolley & Limousine, Mike Maurer, and Kendall and Lois M. Nelson.

Photo Credits:
Title page, pages 28/29 courtesy of U.S. Secret Service; Page 13 © Smithsonian; Pages 14/15, 16/17, 35 © Michael L. Bromley; Pages12/13 © Auburn Cord Duesenberg Museum, Auburn, IN; Cover, pages 19, 20/21, 22, 23, 42/43 © K-8 Images; Page 4 © Theo Westenberger/Getty Images; pages 6 and 24/25 © Getty Images; pages 8/9 and 37 © Douglas Burrows/Getty Images; page 10 © Sebastian Artz/Getty Images; page 31 © Cynthia Johnson/Getty Images

Title page photo: Armored limousines help protect American presidents.

Editor: Frank Sloan

Cover and page design: Nicola Stratford

Notice: The publisher recognizes that some words, model names, and designations mentioned herein are the property of the trademark holder. We use them for identification purposes only. This is not an official publication.

Library of Congress Cataloging-in-Publication Data

Maurer, Tracy, 1965-
  Limousines / Tracy Nelson Maurer.
     p. cm. -- (Roaring rides)
Summary: Discusses the history and current uses of limousines, as well as how they are customized to protect politicians or pamper celebrities.

Includes bibliographical references and index.
  ISBN 1-58952-747-X (hardcover)
  1. Limousines--Juvenile literature. [1. Limousines. 2. Automobiles.]
I. Title. II. Series: Maurer, Tracy, 1965-   Roaring rides.
  TL232.7.M38 2003
  629.222'32--dc21

                                                              2003010019

Printed in the USA

w/w

LIMOUSINES
TABLE OF CONTENTS

CHAPTER ONE	CINDERELLA STORY	4
CHAPTER TWO	CUT AND STRETCHED	18
CHAPTER THREE	BUILT LIKE A TANK	27
CHAPTER FOUR	CHAUFFEURS, NOT DRIVERS	33
CHAPTER FIVE	DRIVEN TO SUCCEED	41
FURTHER READING		45
WEB SITES		45
GLOSSARY		46
INDEX		48

LIMOUSINES

CINDERELLA STORY

Did Cinderella walk to the ball? Did she ride a bike to the ball? Did she magically appear out of thin air on the palace steps? No, no, no.

The wise fairy godmother knew Cinderella had to arrive in style at the ball! No doubt her **exotic** pumpkin coach turned a few heads, just as exotic **limousines** do today.

ROARING FACT

The word *limousine* comes from the Limousin farming region in France. Long ago, shepherds there wore long cloaks in bad weather. Then the word *limousine* became connected with sheltered roofs on local delivery carts. By the early 1900s, long roofs on elegant horseless carriages protected drivers who sat apart from their wealthy passengers, and the name stuck.

A stretch limousine always arrives in style. People outside the limousine wonder about the riders inside. Are they rich? Are they famous? Are they renting the ride just for the night?

ROYAL RIDES

Only the wealthy could afford the dazzling Cinderella-style coaches that were popular in the late 1700s and 1800s. Kings and noblemen hired drivers, called coachmen, to guide and care for their proud teams of horses.

Great Britain's Gold State Coach, built in 1762, still stands ready in the Royal Mews to hitch up to eight horses. Paintings by 18th-century Italian artist Giovanni Cipriani fill the side panels. Heavy gold covers the pillars, wheels, and onboard sculptures. The buggy weighs nearly four tons!

The Royal Mews staff tends to about 100 coaches and carriages, including the lovely Glass Coach that carried Lady Diana Spencer to her wedding.

The Master of the Queen's Horses also oversees Her Majesty's Windsor Grey horses and the fleet of Rolls-Royce limousines kept in the Royal Mews. The world's richest people seem to favor Rolls-Royce, Mercedes-Benz, and Volvo limousines for personal use.

◀ *Only the wealthy own imported limousines like this one, which sells for about $349,000.*

EGYPTIAN LITTERS

Royal coaches were the forerunners of today's limousines. The coachman, alone at the reigns, became the modern **chauffeur**, or hired driver, still separated from passengers. But the idea of arriving in style is far older than Cinderella or the British kings.

In the years somewhere between 1570 and 1070 B.C., early Egyptians showed their power by riding high in a litter—a wooden lounge chair atop long poles carried by lesser nobles. Some of these carrying-chairs were decked out with ebony and gold.

Later, around 300 B.C., the trendy, rich, and dead Egyptians rode to their tombs on beautifully carved wheeled hearses in long funeral processions, or parades. Modern German engineers spent more than 600 hours trying to build a copy of one.

FUNERAL WORK

Like Ancient Egyptian funerals, today's American funerals often include a procession to the burial site with **luxurious** vehicles leading the way.

American coachbuilders, or converters, produce funeral limousines and hearses that look elegant, but not too fancy. Most funeral companies prefer glossy black or white paint on their limousines' exteriors. Some cars fly a funeral flag at the front fender to caution other drivers.

Today in America, a funeral procession often uses a limousine hearse to carry the casket and a stretch limousine for the family of the loved one.

Most state laws require all cars in a funeral procession to use headlights and follow the hearse single file. To show respect, other drivers should not break into the line or turn in front of any of the following cars.

ROADWAY RESPECT

Like earlier coaches and other specialty transportation, modern limousines command respect. Funeral limousines also solve the problem of transporting many people, usually a family, to one place at one time.

Limousines for funerals often hold nine passengers and use six doors. The center doors open to a middle row of seats. These extra doors allow the family members to easily enter and exit the car.

Funeral limousines feature tasteful **upholstery** and thoughtful **amenities** such as tissue holders.

Hearses also use fine fabrics for the interior carpets and drapes, although nobody looks through the windows. Quiet rollers in the floor help move the casket in and out easily.

In some funeral limousines, the middle row faces forward. Fewer funeral limousines position the middle row facing the back seats, an arrangement called vis-à-vis seating.

PEOPLE MOVERS

Stretching a vehicle for the purpose of moving many people began in America for a much livelier reason than funerals.

In 1928, the mechanics of Armbruster & Company in Arkansas cut a Buick into two pieces. They added a middle section with a bench seat. They also put a luggage rack on the roof and a huge storage trunk on the rear.

These first "bandwagons" hauled orchestra members and their instruments to shows across the country. **Politicians** also used these people movers to deliver their messages to voters in the 1930s.

Fancier bandwagons became "airporters" for shuttling tourists from airports to posh hotels. Today's limousine van traces its start to these airporters.

By the Roaring Twenties, coachbuilders from New York to California created fabulous rides for wealthy clients.

LIMOUSINE N° 67

An illustration of one of the earliest limousines built.

Although it wasn't stretched, this elegant 1937 Lincoln Sport Sedan probably served many years as a limousine for its wealthy owner. Note the opposite door handles.

ROARING FACT

As politicians began using stretched cars to travel the country, the term *bandwagon* became associated with election platforms. Now when somebody "jumps on the bandwagon," it means that the person supports an idea or plan.

MANY REASONS TO RIDE

Today, limousines serve many purposes. Some stretch limousines simply carry more people than ordinary vehicles do. These might be funeral limousines or airport limousines. Space and comfort matter more than extreme luxury.

Some stretch limousines focus entirely on luxury. These are stately private cars or the roaring rides hauling wedding parties or other groups ready for a night on the town. Hollywood stars, rock bands, and other **celebrities** often prefer wild luxury cars.

Still other limousines offer luxury, but not for fun. Wealthy **executives** make the most of every minute by working in limousines outfitted with business equipment. Presidents, royalty, diplomats, religious leaders, and businesspeople may choose to armor their limousines with safety systems.

Students often hire stretch limousines to proms and other special events.

LIMOUSINES

CHAPTER TWO

CUT AND STRETCHED

Today, most stretch jobs start with new Cadillacs or Lincolns built just for the specialty car market. General Motors and Ford beef up their pre-limousine engines to deliver more horsepower than ordinary luxury cars. Limousine engines must run gracefully—no jarring between gears and no whining on uphill streets.

Because a limousine often idles for hours, the engine also needs a heavy-duty cooling system and a special air conditioning unit. An overheated engine will stall in traffic—a quick way to make passengers grumpy.

SPARKS FLY

Before cutting apart a nice vehicle, the converter's team rigs special beams under the car to keep the two sections from crashing onto the floor. Tape covers window frames, door handles, and other "keeper" parts. They also strip or cover interior parts.

Sparks fly as the mechanic's electric **abrasion saw** churns through the steel. The piercing wail curls the toes of anyone not wearing earplugs.

A special jig exactly positions the two car sections, stretched apart anywhere from 6 inches (15 cm) to 120 inches (305 cm) in a Ford- or GM-certified shop. Other converters often stretch cars to 200 inches (508 cm).

A vehicle photographed before its limousine conversion.

The stretching operation takes about 20 steps and more than 10 days to finish. Skilled hands carefully create every part to precisely fit the car. One limousine can easily use the talents of more than 400 people.

BRIDGING THE GAP

Expert craftsmen bridge the gap between the front and rear car pieces. Welders dressed in leathers (special fire-resistant gloves and aprons) attach metal parts that lengthen the frame, or chassis.

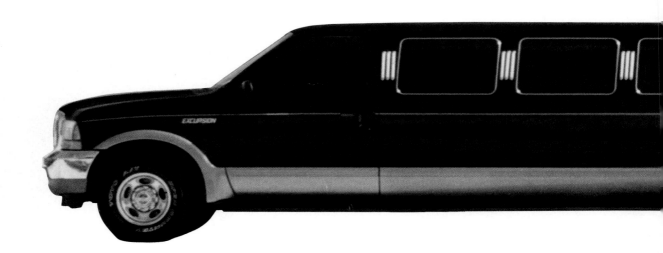

Mechanics build an extra-long fuel system, brake lines, drive shaft, and other parts to fit the car. **Fabricators** use 175-ton presses or even old-fashioned wooden forms to shape the car's new metal skin, such as the side panels and roof.

Electricians add power plants to handle the limousine's extra gadgets, such as a CD or DVD player, surround-sound speaker system, and fax machine.

Painters strip and sand the entire body, even the new parts from the original manufacturer. This gives a flawless finish to their work. They wear **respirators** in a special paint booth where they evenly spray the new paint—layer by layer—onto the metal.

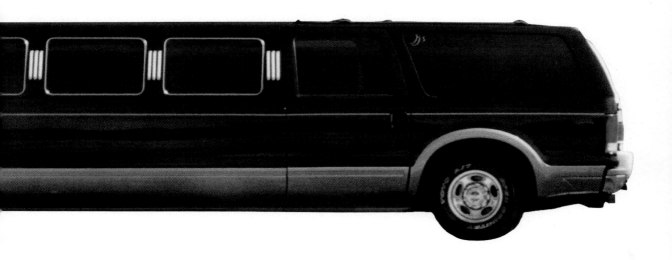

Ford Motor Company and General Motors Corporation certify converters who meet their standards for safety and luxury. Most limousines over 120 inches (305 cm) are not certified.

J-seating – one long, J-shaped seat, most common in 200-inch (508-cm) party cars

Coach lamp – the small, vertical lamps

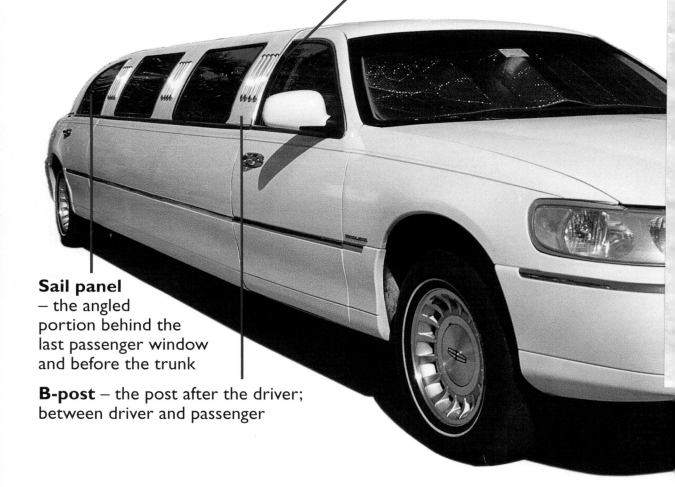

Sail panel – the angled portion behind the last passenger window and before the trunk

B-post – the post after the driver; between driver and passenger

Amenities – Include crystal decanters, entertainment console, laser lighting, telephones, fax machines, hot tubs, etc. Most electrical devices such as CD/DVD, mood lighting, and climate controls are in the overhead panel.

Intercom system – method of communicating with the driver

Privacy divider – a passenger controlled window between the passenger and driver

ROARING FACT

The *Guinness Book of World Records* lists the longest street-legal vehicle at 66-1/2 feet (20.3 m). The 14,000-pound (6,350-kg) two-piece car holds 36 guests. Originally designed by Ultra Coachbuilders for a wealthy sheik, the wild limousine is available for rent from Star Limo in Palos Hills, Illinois.

WHATEVER THEY WANT

Converters custom-build each limousine for the owner. **Livery** companies, which offer chauffeured cars for hire, order cars to please their customers—perhaps adding fax machines, reading lights, and computer outlets for business clients. Or they might order fiber-optic lights, mirrored ceilings, and large beverage centers for party crowds.

A movie called Thunderbirds featured one of the most extreme limousines ever.

Wealthy individuals order **lavish** amenities for their vehicles, too. Imagination and money limit the options. Of course, they expect state-of-the-art entertainment gadgets. They also order everything from hand-stitched goatskin upholstery to oddities like golfing greens, hot tubs, or urinals. Nothing really surprises a converter.

As the "manufacturer of record," the converter must sell safe cars. The National Highway Traffic Safety Administration (NHTSA) expects all stretch limousines to meet federal safety rules, called the Federal Motor Vehicle Safety Standards (FMVSS).

The rules cover impact safety at the front, rear, and sides. They also set fuel system and roof and windshield strength standards.

ROARING FACT

Currently, fewer than 50 companies in the United States convert cars into stretch limousines.

LIMOUSINES

CHAPTER THREE

BUILT LIKE A TANK

Armored limousines have protected bad guys and good guys. The 1930s gangster Al Capone rode in a chauffeured limousine that was custom-built with positions for returning gunfire and a handy escape hatch.

Since President Harry S. Truman, armored limousines have served American presidents. The Secret Service Agency clamped down on presidential limousine construction and use after President John F. Kennedy's **assassination** in 1963.

Now only a few carefully selected people know exactly what protects the American leader. Even fewer people know what the techno-wonders actually cost.

THE CLASSIFIED RIDE

In time for President George W. Bush's **inauguration** in January 2001, the White House took delivery of the presidential armored personnel carrier. This "parade car" was dressed up as a beautiful 2001 Cadillac DeVille.

Taller, longer, and wider than President Bill Clinton's 1993 Fleetwood Brougham, the new seven-seat model stretches out to nearly 270 inches (688 cm). It boasts the latest communications gear and loads of top-secret armor.

Unclassified data from the GM Specialty Vehicle Group claims the car features its patented Night Vision infrared object detection system, plus rare wood accents, rich blue leather and cloth upholstery, a foldaway desktop, halo lighting, reclining rear seats, and a 10-disc CD changer.

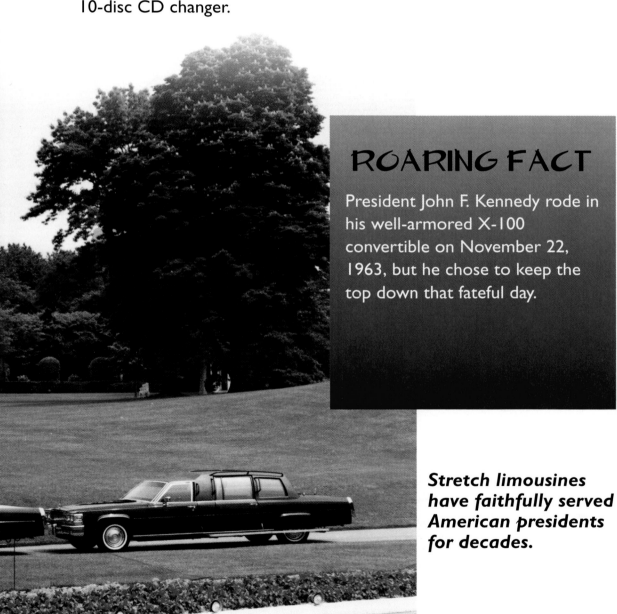

ROARING FACT

President John F. Kennedy rode in his well-armored X-100 convertible on November 22, 1963, but he chose to keep the top down that fateful day.

Stretch limousines have faithfully served American presidents for decades.

READY FOR TROUBLE

Government officials in America face different risks than business leaders in other nations. The armoring company tries to match a limousine's armor to the passenger's possible threat.

Is the client most threatened by assault rifles or handguns? Bombs or hand grenades? Biological or chemical weapons? Kidnapping? Riots? Safety measures exist for each threat.

The armoring team completely strips down the vehicle before installing the new safety systems. Armoring can easily add between 1,200 to 2,500 pounds (544 to 1,134 kg) to the car.

ROARING FACT

Clint Eastwood's movie *In the Line of Fire*, about an aging Secret Service agent, featured a look-alike presidential limousine that was so believable the Secret Service checked on him to make sure he hadn't actually borrowed the real thing.

Added weight and the need for control in high-speed or tricky **maneuvers** also demand a beefed-up suspension system, better brakes, superior lubricants, and perhaps even a stronger, more powerful engine.

A motorcade moves slowly through Washington, D.C. ➤ *keeping the cars in a tight formation. For security reasons, important people don't tell the public if their cars are armored or how they're armored.*

ARMORED OPTIONS

Depending on the danger, armored vehicles may have a combination of upgrades:

- Thick, bullet-proof, splinter-proof glass/polycarbonate windows
- High-strength steel, titanium, composites, and/or Dupont's Kevlar in the doors, floor, firewall, and trunk
- Battery protection
- Radiator protection
- Fuel tank protection
- Reinforced ram bumpers
- Stronger suspension (springs and shock absorbers)
- Better brake systems
- Run-flat tire inserts
- Electric dead bolt locks
- Locking fuel cap
- Satellite telephone
- Inside trunk release
- Auxiliary oxygen supply system
- Seamless welding and gap protection

In America, most armored vehicles start as standard powerhouse models, like Ford Expeditions and Excursions or Chevrolet Suburbans or Tahoes, as well as limousines of all makes and models.

Armoring can cost twice the original purchase price of the vehicle. Prices range from $30,000 to well over $100,000 for a complete Sport-Utility Vehicle.

LIMOUSINES

CHAPTER FOUR

CHAUFFEURS, NOT DRIVERS

Someone other than the limousine owner drives the vehicle.

If that's not a rule carved in stone somewhere, it's certainly the tradition handed down from the days of the coachmen.

Another rule: *Today's professional chauffeur is not a driver.*

Drivers drive semi-trucks, buses, and taxi cabs. The ideal chauffeur combines safe driving skills with all the best of an old-fashioned British butler, the know-how of a mechanic, and the watchful security of a bodyguard. Timing, flexibility, patience, secrecy, and a good sense of direction help, too.

POLITE PROFESSIONALS

Men and women chauffeurs may work for one company, family, or individual. Often, these privately employed chauffeurs maintain the limousines. They fill gas tanks, check fluids, put air in the tires, and schedule regular safety checks.

Private chauffeurs also clean the limousines, sometimes more than twice a day! They polish the brightwork, or chrome and other metal pieces, until the cars sparkle. They might also rake the lawn, pick up the dry cleaning, or run other errands for the boss.

Chauffeurs employed by livery companies focus almost entirely on driving the vehicle and pampering passengers. Like privately employed chauffeurs, they open car doors and help clients safely enter or exit the vehicle—always watching for traffic.

Chauffeurs also load luggage, check airline flights, and hold umbrellas in the rain. Ideal chauffeurs always behave with professional courtesy.

Traditional chauffeur livery, or attire, includes a neatly pressed dark suit, dress shirt, necktie or scarf for women, polished shoes, dark socks or hose, and a cap.

SAFETY FIRST

Chauffeurs practice driving their stretch limousines. Industry leaders claim that professional chauffeurs are at least five times safer than regular drivers are under the same conditions.

Chauffeurs are not perched above the traffic like bus drivers are. They learn to maneuver the long vehicle from their low positions. Chauffeurs often use side mirrors to guide them into tight parking places.

Sometimes chauffeurs jostle for better positions among other limousines at big events. In **motorcades**, they learn to pace the car safely to keep up with the other limousines.

Most state laws require chauffeurs to pass a commercial driver's test like taxi cab drivers do. Many limousine companies also provide special chauffeur training. In addition, companies may check employee backgrounds and test for drug and alcohol use.

ROARING FACT

Drinking and driving never mix! Many people blame chauffeur Henri Paul for the death of Great Britain's Princess Diana. Apparently, he drank alcohol before driving the Princess and her friend. He also drove too fast, especially since he was not the regular chauffeur for that Mercedes-Benz.

Chauffeurs must skillfully back their long limousines into tight spaces like these.

THE FOUR-SECOND RULE

Most traffic accidents happen when one vehicle follows another too closely. Professional driver training programs suggest leaving enough space so that a chauffeur can see the tires of the vehicle ahead.

Other programs recommend using the Four-Second Rule. It works for all drivers:

When the vehicle ahead passes by a fixed object, perhaps a telephone pole or signpost, the driver behind counts slowly to four before passing the same object. A safe driver adds more time in poor weather.

This cushion between vehicles gives the chauffeur time to react to trouble ahead. It also opens the view of the roadway.

Chauffeurs for high-security passengers, such as the President, always scan the view for risks. They also travel in the center lane of a freeway, if possible, to pull out quickly in a crisis.

CLOSE-UP:
Champion Chauffeur

Women chauffeurs handle limousines with flair. Nancy Hollenback cares about her passengers, too. "I feel good about providing a safe form of transportation to those folks who are celebrating," she says.

Nancy and her husband, Russell L. Hollenback, Jr., work as chauffeurs for the fleet of limousines and restored trolleys at Tecumseh Trolley and Limousine in Tecumseh, Michigan. Nancy drives nearly every Saturday during the wedding season, usually from April to October. She likes weddings and shuttling folks around at big events.

Steve Pixley owns the company. He nominated her for the special award because Nancy is a dedicated and caring person. She traveled from Michigan to New York City after September 11, 2001, to help at Ground Zero for six weeks. She provided clinical consulting services to the POPPA (Police Officers Providing Peer Assistance) organization.

NANCY HOLLENBACK
Limousine Digest 2002 Chauffeur of the Year Runner-up

Started as a chauffeur: May 2000, when she saw a trolley at a wedding. "It was awesome and from that moment I knew I wanted to drive one of those, too," Nancy says.

Other occupations: Psychotherapist, social worker, minister, and member of crisis-response team.

Favorite assignment: All kinds! Nancy especially likes when she and her husband work together at the same event, chauffeuring in separate vehicles.

Secret wish: If she owned a limousine, she would surprise people with rides to make their days even more special.

MONEY MATTERS

Chauffeurs work under the glamorous halo of the wealthy, especially if they're privately employed. They generally receive an annual salary. Their perks can be anything from passes to the boss's concert to free living quarters on the estate. A lucky driver might even take home the old limousine when the boss replaces it with a new one.

Most chauffeurs work in the livery business. They meet many kinds of people, from traveling executives to newlyweds. Livery chauffeurs earn from $8 to $10 per hour, plus tips. Tips can top $100 for one assignment.

ROARING FACT

Ford Motor Company estimates that it costs about $60 per hour to rent a Lincoln Town Car Limousine and about $140 per hour to rent a 120-inch (305-cm) stretch limousine for six people, including a 20-percent tip.

LIMOUSINES

CHAPTER FIVE

DRIVEN TO SUCCEED

A livery business usually hits a few bumps and unexpected turns on the road to success. Limousines cost a lot of money to buy. A used limousine starts at about $20,000. New ones can cost well over $75,000. A 2001 200-inch (508-cm) stretch Lincoln Navigator might cost nearly $95,000. License plates and registration fees, not including insurance, can run more than $1,200 each year.

Maintenance isn't cheap, either. A **sedan** can travel between 37,000 and 52,000 miles (59,500 and 83,684 km) in a year. The limousine uses expensive commercial-grade tires that last longer and handle more weight than normal tires. Rowdy passengers damage interiors, too.

MILD TO WILD

Nobody rents an old limousine (unless it's *really* old—like a 1950s classic). Limousine businesses must replace their **fleets** often. Traditional or larger companies with more than 20 cars often snub the super-stretched limousines. They prefer to offer splendid sedans staffed with elegant chauffeur service.

To attract new customers, start-up or contemporary companies often use the funky 200-inch (508-cm) stretch limousines decked in wild amenities. These wonders-on-wheels include stretched SUVS, Hummers, PT Cruisers, and pick-up trucks.

ROARING FACT

Chauffeurs plan extra time in their schedules for young passengers who almost always play with the electronic controls before the car can pull out. Sometimes the eager riders break the gadgets.

Mega-limousines like this one often transport a large group of people for a night on the town.

COLLECTIBLE CONVERSIONS

Neoclassic cars blend classic front-ends with modern passenger areas. They're popular for weddings and other social events.

Collectors treasure truly classic limousines. Some people even collect funeral limousines. A few stunning classic limousines have graced hit movies such as *Driving Miss Daisy* and *Arthur*. Chauffeurs also drive restored trolleys and other unusual collectors' vehicles for limousine companies.

LIMOUSINES UP CLOSE

Renting a limousine is the easiest way to experience the luxury of a chauffeured ride. The National Highway Traffic Safety Administration suggests that high school students work with local limousine companies to promote a zero-tolerance for drinking during prom or other special school events.

Peeking inside limousines annoys passengers. Instead, visit the fabulous American limousines displayed at the Auburn-Cord-Duesenberg Museum in Auburn, Indiana; see the Cinderella-style coaches of the Royal Mews in London; or check out the many limousine shows and displays around the world.

The local library can open the door to more information about these regal vehicles through books, magazines, videos, or Internet access, too.

Further Reading

Long Limousines by Scott P. Werther, Extreme Machines Series, The Rosen Publishing Group, 2002.

Stretch Limousines 1928-2001: Photo Archive by Richard J. Conjalka, Iconografix, 2001.

Stretching It: The Story of the Limousine by Michael L. Bromley and Tom Mazza, Society of Automotive Engineers, Inc., 2002. http://www.stretching-it.com/

Modern Marvels: Limos (television documentary) presented by The History Channel, A&E Television Networks, 2002.

Web Sites

Limousine & Chauffeured Transportation Magazine
http://www.lctmag.com

Limousine Digest Magazine
http://www.limodigest.com

National Highway Traffic Safety Administration
http://www.nhtsa.dot.gov/people/injury/alcohol/zero/page1/idea.html

National Limousine Association
49 S. Maple Ave. in Marlton, NJ (800) 652-7007 (703) 838-2938
http://www.nlaweb.org

Specialty Equipment Market Association
http://www.sema.org

Tecumseh Trolley & Limousine
http://www.michigantrolleys.com

Glossary

abrasion saw (ah BRAY jun   sah) — a tool that uses a grinding blade to cut into metal or other hard materials

amenities (ah MEN i teez) — equipment or features that add comfort or convenience

assassination (ah SASS i nay shun) — murder, usually for political reasons

celebrities (sah LEB ri teez) — famous or well-known people

chauffeur (SHOH fur) — a person hired to drive a vehicle for the car's owner or for a paying passenger

executives (ig ZEK yuh tivz) — people in charge of businesses or organizations

exotic (ig ZOT ik) — unusual or unique

fabricators (FAB ri KAY turz) — people with special skills to make or build things

fleets (FLEETS) — a large group of vehicles operated by a single company

inauguration (in ah gyah RAY shun) — the ceremony that begins a president's new term

lavish (LAV ish) — great amounts; more than normal

limousine (LIM ah zeen) — a chauffeured luxury vehicle that has separate areas for the driver and passengers; the vehicle offers special amenities for the passengers' comfort and pleasure

livery (LIV ah ree) — a company that rents out vehicles; also a special uniform worn by servants

luxurious (lug ZHOOR ee us) — something that is elegant, rich, or expensive; something that is not a necessity

maneuvers (mah NOO vurz) — positions, tricks, or moves

motorcades (MOH tur kaydz) — processions or parades of motor vehicles

neoclassic (nee oh KLASS ik) — something new that looks old

politicians (pol i TISH ehnz) — people who seek or hold public office

respirators (RESS pah ray turz) — masks worn over the mouth and nose to protect against harmful air

sedan (si DAN) — an enclosed automobile body with two or four doors that seats four or more people in two rows of seats

upholstery (up HOL stah ree) — in vehicles, the materials, usually fabric or carpet, used to cushion and cover the interior

Index

abrasion saw   19
airporters   12, 16
amenities   10, 25, 42
armor   27, 28, 30, 32
bandwagons   12, 15
chauffeur   8, 27, 33, 34, 36, 38, 39, 40, 42, 43, 44
converters   9, 19, 24, 25, 26
Egyptians   8, 9
executives   17
fabricators   21
Federal Motor Vehicle Safety Standards (FMVSS)   26

Four-Second Rule   38
funeral   9, 10, 12, 16, 43
hearse   9, 11
Hollenback, Nancy   38, 39
livery company   24, 34, 40, 41
National Highway Traffic Safety Administration (NHTSA)   26, 44
neoclassic   43
respirators   21
Royal Mews   7, 44
Secret Service Agency   27
upholstery   10, 25, 29

About The Author

Tracy Nelson Maurer specializes in nonfiction and business writing. Her most recently published children's books include the RadSports series, also from Rourke Publishing LLC. Tracy lives with her husband Mike and two children near Minneapolis, Minnesota.